RACE FOR YOUR LIFE!

THE TOUR DE FRANCE

BY KATE MIKOLEY

Gareth Stevens PUBLISHING

HOT TOPICS

Please visit our website, www.garethstevens.com. For a free color catalog of all our high-quality books, call toll free 1-800-542-2595 or fax 1-877-542-2596.

Cataloging-in-Publication Data

Names: Mikoley, Kate.
Title: The Tour de France / Kate Mikoley.
Description: New York : Gareth Stevens Publishing, 2021. | Series: Race for your life! | Includes glossary and index.
Identifiers: ISBN 9781538259108 (pbk.) | ISBN 9781538259122 (library bound) | ISBN 9781538259115 (6 pack)
Subjects: LCSH: Tour de France (Bicycle race)–Juvenile literature. | Bicycle racing--France–Juvenile literature.
Classification: LCC GV1049.2.T68 M55 2021 | DDC 796.6'20944–dc23

First Edition

Published in 2021 by
Gareth Stevens Publishing
111 East 14th Street, Suite 349
New York, NY 10003

Designer: Laura Bowen
Editor: Kate Mikoley

Photo credits: Cover, pp. 1–32 (texture) Chatham172/Shutterstock.com; Cover, pp. 1, 9, 19 (cyclists) Chris Graythen/Staff/Velo/Getty Images; pp. 5, 21 ANNE-CHRISTINE POUJOULAT/Contributor/AFP/Getty Images; p. 7 JEFF PACHOUD/Contributor/AFP/Getty Images; p. 11 Jean Catuffe/Contributor/Getty Images Europe/Getty Images; pp. 13, 15, 25, 27 Tim de Waele/Staff/Velo/Getty Images; p. 17 Hu Chengwei/Stringer/Velo/Getty Images; p. 21 ullstein bild Dtl./Contributor/ullstein bild/Getty Images, p. 23 DAVID STOCKMAN/Contributor/AFP/Getty Images; p. 29 Justin Setterfeld/Staff/Velo/Getty Images.

Printed in the United States of America

CPSIA compliance information: Batch #CS20GS: For further information contact Gareth Stevens, New York, New York at 1-800-542-2595.

CONTENTS

OFF TO FRANCE

Every year, the world's best bike riders head to France. There, they take part in the world's most famous bike race—the Tour de France. Over more than 20 days, the race covers more than 2,000 miles (3,219 km)!

FEARLESS FACTS

The sport of riding a bicycle is called cycling. **Athletes** in the sport are called cyclists.

As the name suggests, the Tour de France happens mainly in France. However, parts of the race sometimes go into other countries in Europe. **Millions** of people watch from the side of the road. Even more watch the race on TV.

FEARLESS FACTS

Cyclists come from all over for the Tour de France. So do **spectators**! In 2019, about 20 percent of people watching in person were from countries other than France.

STAGE TIME

The race happens over 23 days, with two rest days. Twenty-one days are spent racing. Each day's part of the race is called a stage. Some stages are flat. Others are steep. The first cyclist to finish each day is that day's stage winner.

FEARLESS FACTS

Some stages of the Tour de France are time trials. These are parts of the race where cyclists race against the clock.

THE YELLOW JERSEY

Each day, one racer wears a yellow **jersey**. This is the person who's in the lead at the start of that day. To figure out who this is, racers' times from each stage are added together. The cyclist with the fastest total time wears the jersey.

FEARLESS FACTS

The yellow jersey is often called by its French name, the *maillot jaune*.

WINNING THE RACE

The overall winner of the Tour de France isn't necessarily the person who crosses the finish line first on the last day of the race. The person with the fastest time for all stages added together is the winner.

FEARLESS FACTS

There are extra contests within the whole race. The best **sprinter** gets to wear a green jersey. The person who does best on hills wears a polka dot jersey!

A TEAM SPORT

Even though there's only one overall winner in the Tour de France, it's a team sport. Each cyclist on a team has an important role, or part to play. All teammates work together to help their team leader win the race.

FEARLESS FACTS

Even though there's only one winner, most leaders know they can't win without the help of their team!

One key position in the team is the *domestique*. This person is a helper. Throughout the race, different people act as the domestique, even the leader. They may pass out water or ride in a certain spot to make the stage easier for others.

FEARLESS FACTS

During flat stages, teammates may work together to help their best sprinter win the stage—even if that's not the teammate aiming to win the whole race!

Teams use techniques, or methods, to win. A domestique may sprint ahead. The members of other teams then want to catch up. When they do, another domestique sprints ahead. The idea is to tire out other teams so the leader can race ahead and win.

FEARLESS FACTS

Drafting is another important technique. It's when one person rides close behind another. This makes the ride easier because the person in front blocks the wind.

TOUR HISTORY

The first Tour de France happened in 1903. It was set up by Henri Desgrange and his sports newspaper. The first race had only six stages, but they were longer than today's stages. Racers didn't ride in teams or even wear helmets!

FEARLESS FACTS

The winner of the first Tour de France was Maurice Garin. Altogether, the race took him more than 95 hours.

The yellow jersey worn by race leaders today wasn't part of the race until 1919. Spectators couldn't always tell who was winning the race. To make it easier, Desgrange decided the leader would wear the yellow jersey.

FEARLESS FACTS

Yellow is an easy color to spot, but that's not why it was chosen for the jersey. Desgrange's newspaper was printed on yellow paper. The color was chosen to honor it.

BIKE BASICS

For a race like the Tour de France, any old bike won't do. In fact, most cyclists in the race use three different kinds of bikes. One is for time trials, one is for flat stages, and one is for the steep parts of the race.

FEARLESS FACTS

Each type of bike is built to be the fastest for its kind of riding. Bikes used for steep climbs are extra light so the rider isn't carrying unnecessary weight.

WOMEN ON THE ROUTE

As of 2019, only men race the Tour de France. In 2015, a group of women rode the **route**, starting the day before the race began. This continued in following years, **promoting** equal rights for women and showing that women can do the race.

FEARLESS FACTS

The pack of racers in a cycling race is called a peloton.

WANT TO RIDE?

Do you have what it takes to ride thousands of miles over challenging terrain and wear the yellow jersey? If you think you'd like to race in the Tour de France someday, start learning about bike skills and safety now!

FEARLESS FACTS

In the Tour de France, the lead rider under 25 years old wears a white jersey. This shows off the best young rider.

RULES TO FOLLOW

Tour de France cyclists must:

- ALWAYS WEAR A HELMET
- WEAR THEIR TEAM'S OFFICIAL OUTFIT UNLESS THEY'VE EARNED A SPECIAL JERSEY
- HAVE PROVIDED NUMBER PLATES SHOWING ON THE SIDES OF THE BIKE
- WEAR OFFICIAL NUMBERS ATTACHED TO THEIR UNIFORM
- SIGN IN BEFORE EACH STAGE

FOR MORE INFORMATION

BOOKS

Brundle, Joanna. *The Scale of Famous Journeys.* New York, NY: Crabtree Publishing Company, 2020.

Hellebuyck, Adam and Laura Deimel. *Tour de France.* Ann Arbor, MI: Cherry Lake Publishing, 2020.

Shea, Therese. *All About Bicycles.* New York, NY: Britannica Educational Publishing, 2017.

WEBSITES

Bike Safety
kidshealth.org/en/kids/bike-safety.html?ref=search
Learn how to stay safe on your bike here.

Cycling
www.dkfindout.com/us/sports/cycling/
Check out this website to learn more about the sport of cycling.

Tour de France
www.letour.fr/en/
Keep up with the latest happenings about the Tour de France on its official website.

GLOSSARY

athlete: someone who is physically fit and takes part in sporting events

jersey: a shirt worn in a sporting event

million: a thousand thousands, or 1,000,000

promote: to help something happen, develop, or increase

route: a course that people travel

spectator: someone watching a sporting event

sprinter: a cyclist who is good at sprinting, or riding very fast for parts of a race

INDEX